HARCOURT, INC.

Orlando

Austin

New York

San Diego

Toronto

London

GREETINGS

Hugo Claus

SELECTED POEMS

Translated from the Dutch by John Irons

GREETINGS

www.HarcourtBooks.com

Translation of this book is funded by the Flemish Literature Fund
(Vlaams Fonds voon de Letteren, www.vfl.Ge).

Library of Congress Cataloging-in-Publication Data
Claus, Hugo, 1929-
[Poems. English. Selections.]
Greetings : selected poems / Hugo Claus; translated from the Dutch
(Belgium) by John Irons.—1st ed.
p. cm.
Includes bibliographical references.
1. Claus, Hugo, 1929—Translations into English. I. Irons, John, 1942- II. Title.
PT6410.C553A25 2004
839.3'1164—dc22 2005015236
ISBN-13: 978-0151-00900-8
ISBN-10: 0-15-100900-7

Text set in Memphis Light
Designed by Scott Piehl

Printed in the United States of America

First edition
K J I H G F E D C B A

CONTENTS

GREETINGS

ABOUT YOU

The child strangles a little crow
Fingers make their groping ways
The dew makes the rubble glow
The dune is all ablaze
The hours chase each other
The days shorten with each season
The weeks catch up with one another
The months wilt and wither
The year is slighter than a butterfly
Slighter than the spider that brings
Evening hope and morning rue

Everywhere all of this because of you.

WITHOUT FORM OF PROCESS

All of us have known for centuries
that the moon hangs on only by a wire
to the heavens, to hell, or to the void.
That night's blue paint
spread thick between the streets
will envelop you like a blue gown
when you make your way home this evening,
late idlers, theater and lecture addicts,
knights of the night, living souls,
and that the night soon will wash away
like cheap blue ink when years have passed
and that then the pale, pink skin of
the heavens, of hell, or of the void
will show through and never fade,
the pink void like the soft, salt sex
of a girl
and that then the heavens, hell, and the void
will dry up, rot, and waste away
like old loves, bad habits,
the clap, dependable furniture, and the
bunkers from before fourteen eighteen, must die,
without anyone's help, in a corner, on a stone in the sand
must die like crafty old crabs.

*

In the autumns and the wet winters
there are days when nothing happens
indoors. Only the breaking of the past,
like the breaking of a past day set in glass,
like the melting of pieces of pond-ice,
so that it's done for, the past, it's done for.
But the past and the present do not give up,
they turn in a horse-walk, take each other's hand
and once more become weeks and months and finally
    seasons.
There are days
when all the clocks of all the towers in the country
are half an hour slow,
and not one of the winter people has noticed,
and the lost half hours no one saved
ride through town and village, unseen, behind the
streetcars and
the carthorses and join together as a new day,
like snow forms an ice-man
into an ice-day for the lonely,
for whom all evenings are holy
like this one.

*

Who smokes his pipe by the fireplace?
Who likes to dance, drink, and play cards?
Father does.
Don't swear. God sees you.
Who takes care of her plenteous brood
and is loved by everyone?
Mother does.
Where are we more at ease
than with our very best friends?
And sleep, embrace, caress, death, uncover and cremate
your lady friend in spirals of salt
your lady friend gnawed full of holes, death.

THE JOYOUS AND UNFORESEEN WEEK

You who are amazed at the 100-times repeated
and identically experienced,
You who want the truth (to gut
her, skin her, sell her skin dear)
yes, you who get through the week
as if it had nothing to do with you,
you listen to how in the maternal dark
of a Saturday you relate (with your hand to your mouth)
(with your voice in your throat): I was born
not out of a vagina but
by a cesarean.

AT HOME

Father was eating partridge and Mother was out
and I and Joris were talking about murders
and getaways and on what trains
when the sun rolled into our attic
and lay there gleaming in the hay.
Father swore and said: God sees me.
Joris made his getaway
and I went on playing with the trains
which ran on electricity across the floor
between posts.

EXERCISES

With the ball of the laughing children against the wall,
With the evening game of hide-and-seek against the wall,

With the lakes in the sea,
With the birds on the watery dikes against the wall,

With the boats, the penitents, the priests,
With the houses of pleasure, the strange countries on the map,
With the art-makers, the books, the friends against the wall,

With evening and night in one bag against the wall,
With the days in a row and boundless against the wall,

And I don't take it seriously
When tomorrow or the day after
You, my darling, childlike
As a lonely child playing seriously,

Will have taken that sponge wall, that smoke wall,
That squat wall, that incandescent wall,

and pulled apart and broken and destroyed it.

Let me tell you once again,
I don't take it seriously
Whatever happens
In this suddenly open and suddenly empty stubble field
That you will leave behind.

*

I have just met Despair with his top hat and white waistcoat
And striped trousers and snubbed him.
At each encounter he conceals his scratches,
But sooner or later he makes up for lost time.

But I flat-out ridicule poor Mrs. Sooner-or-Later
For—
Now—
Free of all birds, the children of summer have been let out.
The grass moves; the land lies ready in a thousand folds;
The streets surge;
And the streetcars filled with wind cross the humped bridges.
And I call you my thirteen-year-old bride,
My breath on the window-pane, my boat, my privateer's
        booty.
I call to you and, across the houses and the towns
And the scarecrows,
I tie new snares in your yellow hair;
And you, you let it happen.

One of these days I will stand once more
ransacked in front of you in the Zuidpark;
We will go down the stairs together;
Happily stroke the stone lions;
Laugh very loud when we see Them;
Mr. Despair and Mrs. Sooner-or-Later;
And when They approach (for approach They will)
We will exorcise them with violent new gestures.

*

Day sits in its cage,
And I sit in my shirt.

The wind tugs at the winter windowpanes,
The wind sniffs the shop windows,
The girls polish the faces of the streets
Before they make love on Friday evening,
And the dunes have subsided.

And thinking of my blond, bleeding love
I say to my neighbor:
    It won't last,
    She threatens me with the wind,
    And after all I'm twenty
    And he's fourteen thousand years old!

But my neighbor in his shirt says:
You will never win.

I say:
    I'll throw the wind through the shop window,
    Pick it up and stomp it to pieces
    And throw him to the squint-eyed girls
    Who are never satisfied from making love.

But my neighbor in his shirt
While looking at his neighbor in the stained mirror
Says sadly: You can't win.

Day sits in its cage squeezed by hours.

SAYINGS

1

The sea is high, the world blue.
New life grows in me.
I want to kill the dogs.

2

Like the tired horseman in the swamp
Someone rides in me
And calls me: stony and sandy desert.

3

Words are uninhabitable houses.
My voice is water.
I am of the white race and unmarried.

4

The valley is stained with ravens.
I have heard the new season.
My mother has not yet died.

PICTURE PUZZLE

The clothes are hanging by the window.
Where is the undressed man
Who in his hand will hold
The lit lamp over the dark room-land?

Turned up his shoes? Among the non-Jews,
The murderers, the dog-tamers
Grave desecraters?

Where in the midst of the pious callosity
are as violent life
The lamp, the man, the light?

FIFTIES

Kulak, teeny-bopper, young blood, pimp,
all of that and more and less.
Back then you said about a woman
that she was like a shrub bird.
Not so much nowadays.
Bearded, churlish, cordial, cadging.
Back then you held your rhyme inside
under your breath.
King, charlatan, angel, lackey,
composite of alter egos.
Once you were him, although sloppily.
Back then you scavenged for coins in the gutter,
that was also called poetry
as were shot glasses, shouting, the last cigarette butts,
all the rest were shady dealings, tainted.
Full of fragments and echoes.
Back then boy-wonder
they butchered the language
but it didn't make a difference.
Back then Vespas capsized
and people lisped unashamedly
about the face of beauty,
gazed on the horizon and on backsides,
shouting hellaciously about everything else.
Mimicry, metaphor, and melopoeia
and you and you and you bobbed along
with *out of the blue*

the Katzenjammer toowhoo!
Machines were uncontrollable incomprehensible
thus: holy.
Back then a law full of rasters was gradually laid
on the tongue, one forbade roses,
but crept cautiously along the palisade
of poetry, oh cherished injury,
and suddenly Chet Baker was toothless.

CHET BAKER SINGS

When I see you walking / and you're not there
I see what you don't see /

I can't *get along without you very well* /
Sleep six times more
and all fingers ready at your soft crater /
and you weren't there /

When I saw you walking / and you're not there /
do you also have that emptiness in your groin? /
did you raise your little paw, little she-goat, near de Bijenkorf
and your hoof scratched your left ear /

Was it music that we once made? /
The emptiness is a sound
when no one whistles at you / Is it over? /

Lady is Cancer, in love with her past
(backwards, backwards) /
In the same time of our lives
she wants to play the widow

I said something like: but lady
                like: do you owe me something perhaps?
No, she said, not something, everything, no she didn't say
    that /
and backwards / her scales soon choke
her flesh / if she was still there /

and then? and then? and then?
Then she pointed to her heart and to my eyes

and I see her walking, my white night tonight /
and I in rooms: dog and hunger /

IN MEMORY OF FERDI

In the Paris which I now hate,
in rooms that scorched in '55,
we were hungry then,
you went barebreasted that summer—
Your lips: scornful of everyone else.

You now in the night as in water
and I—do you believe me?—sleepless, senseless.
You who made velvet fronds
in what I now have to call "back then."

You still distract my thoughts of you
which bubble and babble away
in this shaky canto for a slim, faded lady.

Ah, the falseness of my remorse
and the distraught, wandering course
of my makeshift present time
with you in many skins, fleshy flowers
in the bygone, bygone zone.

APRIL IN PARIS

(in 1951
when Charlie Parker was still alive)

The undulating bars of Avenue des Champs

oh high pale fields
there a child dances losing
helplessly all winter notes of sorrow and
death and hunger Goodbye hello gray days
among the plaster notes oh song of the parks

yes we are lost we want
rain and hail
not to return to that slow land
of oxen and potato fields and when I was in the polders
I would set fire to three villages there
and plant a tree there and build a house
and go to live there and blow on a horn
so the crows passed it on
so the ravens on fire flew out of the trees
so the young wood split and the land
trembled in furrows but I am in the light
you see me come and say hello
April day

Elysées and the street ends in a calm river
ends as one: hello Charlie how are you?

as if the summer comes without suspicion without
cautious hands
not curbed not prevented by
—I already know I knew it I have
the whole time (time with hips and organs) known it—
the cautious hands of knowledge and memory and
premature death and

so I was no more there tomorrow in the summer
yes ends as a: hello Charlie go and lie in the sand
the king drinks oh corals and ores
in me spattered apart

elysées

lower now and tender as the cobweb the slime of the
        hay-spider
like the colored spotted pupil of a strong green animal

ah a hundred shrubs
blossoming edge of things
while in

elysées

—hello Charlie blood-stained goshawk whistle
that stalks my movements and makes me walk with a
        new face
with an animal look through the summer evening street—

the three women of the morning clamber on each other
and the lanterns go out
while in the golden plain
the gray night-woman flees from the gardens
and the cardinal pees into the hedges.

and yes listen
we greet each other
hello king
hello prince

and the conversation of the royalists lights up
our sleeping house and day takes cover
in the stumbling stones

the president will die

thus does the very first newspaper vendor call to us
this too we will survive once more

the night is a woman
oh a hundred thousand lips
and with the morning two identical mournful Chinamen
enter our waking house
and say unheard sentences with their hands
about castles or prisons
(they look through the bars of their fingers)

and we in this white and everyday Paris
we become water and flow open
and all at once have moved houses
and no longer find the morning and think in Chinese
and dive under bridges and are the Seine

supposing the morning was Oriental
supposing cheng-wa now was: the sun rises
or was: the sun sets
or was: a large fish or fishfeed
or was: we want bread and have sleep

the hit-sick fingers of the day
stroke open the face of the streets

the day is another woman
oh a hundred thousand lips.

1965

(in answer to a survey in
De Standaard *concerning the previous year)*

Year of atrocities, year of cathode-ray tube and stock market
    report,
Year of milk and honey if you're asleep,
Year that sticks in your stomach if you're awake,
Sweet year, good year for sleepwalkers,
Year in which 25 billion Belgian francs went to NATO
for flags, tanks, and planes
    (midges in the limitless clouds of death)
Year of Mobutu, we send him cents and assistants
    that will blossom into percentages,
Year of the Voerstreek which people want to save as a
    language
    that you only read in ads,
Year of the highway for ever faster cattle,
Year of the fungus in the Belgian braincase,
Year that licked at the trough of folklore,
Year (luckily far away from our savings stocking
              and our folk dancing)
    of the escalation there where the children gray
        with fear
    dig themselves into the mud
    (Give them this day our daily napalm
    and later our canned food and later our prayers)
Year that freezes the smile.

It was in that year I went to live in a village
with books, a wife and a child
who grows
while I talk about the tigers in the East.

STILL NOW

I

Still now, on the gallows today, a rag in her mouth,
she who wakes with swollen lips, her eyes still closed,
she was something I knew and have since lost and how,
but how did I lose her, how does a drunk dog bark?

II

Still now, her face as the moon and her body as the moon
young, bitter young, with those breasts and buttocks and
those ribs
Earlier you had love's darts, you truly felt them there,
they stung, you thought, that bright full moon of hers.

III

Still now her bitten nails, her bruised nipples,
her smooth buttocks between which she smiles her vertical
smile
and she who reviled metaphysics said: "Oh, sweetie,
in each cell of your sperm sits God and his mother."

IV

Still now the stripes scratches stains tattoos,
all wounds of love beneath her flimsy frock,
and I fear this will remain, this nasty underhand
scratching and clawing for her undersize no-man's-land.

V

Still now, completely still she lay excessively alone,
crosswise abandoned and with paralyzed palate,
and I, just as motionless in my cell, I heard them,
the tinkling chains around her left ankle.

VI

Still now I know how, tired and limp after languid lovemaking,
she leaned her head forward almost shyly in the morning,
a duck that slid across the lake and sipped at the water
and then dipped down to me and bit and then never again.

VII

Still now I bind her jet-black hair in horny
crests and spears and spines and worship her as
totem and cross in my house which clumsily and hastily
turns into a temple to Love, the furtive goddess.

VIII

Still now all those rooms and nights and creamily nude
and all that sleep after and before and the scent of hay.
How she snored when I asked if she was happy now
and how she caressed the plump pillow next to me.

IX

Still now her limbs, all four busy, done in,
and her newly washed hair over her warm cheeks,
then she grasped my neck with her ankles, giggling
    executioner,
beheaded she offered me her cool glistening wound.

X

Still now I hoist a flag and raise my arms aloft
and shout "Comrade." But she was the one who
    surrendered.
For on the battlefield I heard her stammeringly rave
with her mother's accent, obscene syllables.

XI

Still now, when I am on the point of crossing over
to that other life, she leads me as through black water
and peers and leers at me through her dangerous lashes
and laughs when dripping-wet I clamber up to her golden
    verge.

XII

Still now her whole body is crimson and glistening with
    sweat
and her openings slippery with baby oil.
Yet what I know of her remains a curious gesture,
echoless, full of bitterness, chance, and regret.

XIII

Still now I forget the gods and their ministers,
it is she who shatters, sentences, and forgets me,
she of all seasons but above all of winter
for she grows more beautiful and cold as I continue dying.

XIV

Still now among all women there is not one like her,
not one whose savage mouth has so amazed me.
My besotted soul would describe her if it could
but it was ravaged by all that is hers.

XV

Still now how she trembled with tiredness and whispered:
"Why are you doing this? I'll never let you go again, my king."
There was no colder prince than I and recklessly
I let her see how the king wept from his one eye.

XVI

Still now when I dare to think of my lost bride
I quiver when I think of who's plucking her now,
my wandering oleander of a bride who time and time
again pulls up the weed that is me from her pleasure
      garden.

XVII

Still now while the bees of death swarm around me
I taste the honey of her belly and hear the humming
of her coming and stare at the moist pink
leaves of her mobile flesh-eating flower.

XVIII

Still now our wide bed that smells of her and her armpits,
our pale bed shat upon by the birds of the world.
At the bird market she said: "I want that one, that wild one
      there,
that keeps tapping its beak against her tit."

XIX

Still now, how she resisted and refused my mouth,
and only when I floored her with my nails in her breast
lay null and void and then, while I slept drunk on her
    abundance,
poked me up again like a hearth long since thought
    extinguished.

XX

Still now her mobile breast that lay there in my hands
and her lips thickened by my tooth-bites
and her bitten nails and bruised nipples,
and how she squinted in the angry morning light.

XXI

Still now I imagine that she, in the narrow space of time
between me and the polar night, has been the stars,
the grass, the cockroaches, the fruits, and the worms
and that I accepted this and that it still delights me.

XXII

Still now, how to describe her hair, to what can I compare her?
Until I'm in my grave I'll arrange her and tint
and spoil her and breathlessly blow her back to life
with my tiresome moaning, my nerve-racking whining.

XXIII

Still now her eyes with the mascara and the eye-shadow
and the scarlet lobes of her ears pierced.
"I have a fever," she says, "I can't any more, I'll kill
you, your fingers, no one else ever, nowhere, never."

XXIV

Still now she'll be nineteen, though she drinks a lot,
and too many tears have traced furrows over her
cheeks, war-paint and camouflage,
the mold and the rigorous frost of her life without me.

XXV

Still now if I should find her again like a fairy tale
of the moon after rain and lick once more her toes,
on my feet once more with my heart of stone I'm afraid a
weird weak song might be awoke like one by Cole Porter.

XXVI

Still now, she more than the water in her curious body
a salt lake on which a duck would drift and stick
and I was that duck with a dick—hear me quack!—and she
being a lake rocked me on the waves or pretended to.

XXVII

Still now if I were to see her again with that nearsighted look,
heavier in the hips and broader in the beam,
I would, I think, embrace her, drink from her again,
no drone would be busier more joyful more supple.

XXVIII

Still now while I sit entangled and entwined in her
the Destroyer is at work scorching humanity.
Respectable humans have lost their way
as after a fight without weapons and without winners.

Still now riveted in her fetters and with the bloody nose
of lovers I say, filled with her blossoming spring:
"Death, torture the earth no longer, do not wait, dear death,
for me to come, but do as she does and strike now!"

STATUE IN OSTEND

Once she lay facing the sea
her heavenly rift ready.

Groups of youths threw stones at her eyes
or painted her belly scarlet.

Men from the local authorities demanded an explanation,
trembling because her—and their—shame was visible.
"For, gentlemen, is this,
for the many visitors
who come to play roulette in our city,
a statue of our women,
this heated flesh, this vagabond woman?"

She is known as fat Mathilda.
She now lies low, in a public garden,
and is no longer touched.
As if stunned repugnance stalls in her proximity,
as if the gleaming of her flanks is frightening.

She lies out of range of the gapers,
she rouses the boulder in their crotch
and in their gaze the prayer: "Oh, blessed one, oh if only
I could ride you unpunished."

GISTEL-BIJ-BRUGGE

The village of cows and willows,
The tower and rows of rhododendrons.

In a curtain of rain
And in a fold of sky and in the light
Sits the bronze mayor soldered to his bronze palms.

Moss from the palm of your hand,
Rain from the white of your eye.
Hedge-tops of your eyelashes,
Ochre hills of your breasts,
And the folds of the entire land of your body.

And the ringed bulls call
Through the ring of hay to the open fields,
But you do not hear the nearby cows.

ON THE QUAY

1

The winter wreaths hang in the boats
In the dusk those almost dead
Come ashore.

The month slowly moving changes
While in the October wind the boats begin to fail

I hear the dogs
The sea is high and a hundred roofs wide
And I still have to get over it

A coly bird against the tattered windows
Of a gutted hotel
(On whose walls is written in chalk:
Maria sleeps with Catherine and Willem the fool is a fool)

The season of love leaves gashes behind in October.

2

The girl from the mine keeps watch.
Her never-healed hands in her lap,
The baskets with herring and shrimps and crabs
And jellyfish and sand.
The last of the fishermen climb the stone quays
And have their silent scanty say.

Hear their shrill names.
Think of the bastards of the A.O. 24
Which the female fish gorge themselves on.
See the meadows of the ruttish land behind the dikes.

In the shed where the young apprentices screw
Under the sails
Hang straight rows of eel.

A glass man falls out of a pub and breaks.

THE DISEASE OF VAN DER GOES

Magistrates, soldiers, flag-decked city, garlanded gallows,
Charles the Bold comes to Ghent,
the people sob at the scene of the Passion,
at the duke's majesty,
at his imperious gaze.

The smoky alleyways, the stench of the rabble,
the leprous streets
are cordoned off, deadened
by panels with altar naves, spring gardens
painted in exquisite perspective
by Hugo van der Goes.

Remember who sweated and stank and screamed for his
        father—
with rotten teeth, wheezing, *Eli, Eli,*
        blue nails, red eyes, he was
once a child like one painted by Van der Goes:
a worm packed in a membrane,
in dirty snow melting in the hay
        (and behind it, among cows dancing
        in misery: weavers, peasants, laborers).

The holy child is lit from below
by a footlight.
On the evil mysteries that conceal the plague
      on the inexplicable
      impatient push for the Last Judgment
lightly the good-giver lifts the curtain.
(Birth and death: theater)

.

IN FLANDERS FIELDS

Here the soil is most rank.
Even after all these years without dung
you could raise a prize death leek here.

The English veterans are getting scarce.
Every year they point to their yet scarcer friends:
Hill Sixty, Hill Sixty-One, Poelkapelle.

In Flanders Fields the threshers
draw ever-smaller circles around the twisting trenches
of hardened sandbags, the entrails of death.

The local butter
tastes of poppies.

MEMORIAL STATUE IN WEST FLANDERS

The grazing of the cattle close by.
The farmer sitting in the shadow of the pale statue.
The trees bending in the sea breeze.

His parents have bought the plot of land
where he stuck in mud up to his jawbone.
He was a promising student.
"Something to do with math," the farmer says.

The statue was made from a school photo.
"Two years later his parents died, too," says the farmer.
"It's getting nippy. I'll just go and milk the goats."

Somewhere another cartilage
Eaten away by the acid of the polderland soil,
a son without children,
staring guiltily, as at his geometry book,
at his grave in the grass.

ANTHROPOLOGICAL

This people of which it is said
that it moves between two poles,
the lewd and the devout,

believes less in the hereafter
than in its daily groats.

This people will give alms on Sundays
to the pope or the negroes,

or with incense honor the statue
of the Priest of Ars who stank of the poor,

but mostly this people flatters with money and prayers,
fearing the lean years,
its docile rulers, the brokers.

.

THE FARMERS

Thirty pigs, fifteen cows, one tractor 75 HP,
one TV, fifty chickens, no children.
    (We would have liked to, Sir,
    but we don't like going to the doctor,
    for if anything happens to the missus, Sir,
    who takes care of the livestock?)

The residences "Wind-child," "Spring Breeze," "Bambino"
stand planted in their fields.
Through their rye and oats the Flemish Tourist Board
walks along the recommended footpaths.

On Sundays, after mass, they move,
shaven, in their shirts, transformed, unaccustomed, across
    their fields
staring at the earth that they do not see during the week
through the nearsighted delving and scrabbling.

Potatoes with bacon every day of the week
and on special days a chicken from the deep-freezer.
When the air boils and the crows gawk, they drink seven
gulps of stallion ale
leaning against the oil tank next to the gable.

They only tremble after a day of upper-arm lifting when
    haymaking,
or when the deposit book of the municipal credit is being
filled in. ("Three to three and a half per cent. Is that safe?
The notary says it is. But if anything happens,
Sir?")

Does the ringing of the village bells protect them
from their fate? Against the evil eye three bats are nailed
    while still alive against the
    barn door.

WEST FLANDERS

Sparse song dark thread
Land like a sheet
That sinks

Springland of hooves and milk
And children of willow

Fever and summerland when the sun
Makes its young in the corn

Blond fencing
With the deaf-mute farmers by the dead firesides
Who pray "May God forgive us for
What he has done to us."

With the fishermen who burn on their boats
With the spotted animals the foaming women
That sink

Land you break into me. My eyes are shards
I in Ithaca with holes in my skin
I borrow your air in my words
Your bushes your lime trees hide in my language

My letters are: West Flanders dune and polder

I drown in you
Land you become a gong in my skull and sometimes
Later in the harbors
A conch: May and beetle Dim light
Earth.

HOME

(for Roger Raveel)

I

As I walk the houses shut.
My hand mows, the world tips,
Violence waits on the road
But I do not reach out nor do I resist.

Would a triple jump
Save me from my tangle?
I would rather see a lukewarm dome
Sink further over my ears,
Or electrodes wind closer
To my temples each year
And increase their charge, unnoticed, a soft water.

Come in,
Take off your coat,
change your manners,
ignore the cat,
say something.
The room is in flower
and under the spell of treacherous things
like: your name, your sentences, memories.

In the branches the dove waits, still as death,
For the lightning already lurking in the landscape
That will strike her, in the eyes.

The land, its organs in order,
The light that spreads out variously
Have trapped us, who escapes?
One dies deservedly in disarray.

And see my father standing
peeing into the hedge
leaving the earth unscathed
where his slippers are.
Father does not want to read
any scriptural signs in the spring vegetables
and does not grumble about the empty,
peevish nature of the world
that sits immovably between his ears.

II

"The grass in my yard grows profusely enough
And that God I only knew from hearsay
When in a shattered prism I saw
Our cat lying there, curled up
And I bent down to stroke her
That God touched my jawbone
And put it out of joint.
Since then my face sits squeezed
In a frame and pushed to one side.
My eyes: black-scorched shutters.
So far I do not pray
But I fear it won't last much longer.
Therefore: I have heard about colors
          that numb thought.
Therefore: so that I do not stay stuck
          in this narrow, dingy street

Oh paint me blue
So the sinister, bitter force in my head weakens
Before the deathblow comes!"

Yard and spring. The season with its greenery has
Besieged and possessed the earth outside.
The stones moult
In the light, plenty of calm and fanciful branches.
Flat expanses of meadow. Little, but everything. One simple law:
What thrives is good.

The rest: the yearning for soot and sand and ash
Blows away.

III

The simple sky
That lights up the earth.

The path that leads our footsteps
And inside our track: a dotted line to the end.

Nature: bordered
The land: bounded
By the colors of salmon and metal.

The poles that surge as you move.
The field of saffron reflected.

The dove behind wire.
The mouse-gray on the floor of the cage
Is the old seed.

Speckled and striped.
The world seems caught in a grid.
Your gaze passes through the pattern into a hole,
Flecked, almost flattened out,
The hole is a mirror.

The simplicity of a bucket.

And finally, awake, present,
Bounded by walls of gradual lines,
Turning on his motionless axis,
The man bending down to his bucket.

Here. An own world almost.

CALIGULA

Where later resedas and radishes flower
That is in May and in a garden and along the tracks
Of a rural train
Now
In the freezing wind and in December
In the wind without light without shepherds without birds
Without a single chance a foal has frozen to death.

I have brought it with me and placed it under glass
And watch through the days and hours
(Which go alongside me on the broad path
Of this existence which indeed
Is perpetrated in sin and senselessly)
And wait until the grateful
Thawed-out foal speaks its first word to me.

A RENDEZVOUS

You say once more: Hello and Good Evening.
Your words come with the crooked walk
Of the tortoise up to me in the kitchen.
The fourteen monkeys in the garden
Stand next to each other screaming in the rain
Hiding under the rhubarb leaves.

The wire that bangs against the smoke-blackened wall
When it blows very hard.
The last cigarette. The smoke. The ash.
We still have thirty years to live
And then centuries more.

The elevator starts. The footsteps in the hallway.
I shiver. You are sitting behind bars now
And will not walk past me any more.

MONTALE'S "SMALL TESTAMENT"

For Harry

What lights up the skullcap
of my thoughts at night like a will-o'-the-wisp—
the mother-of-pearl trail of the snail
or the glittering dust of pulverized glass—
is no church light, no office light
left on
by a clerk, a red or a black.

Only this rainbow, this iris
can I leave for you.
Only the evidence of a faith
that was assaulted,
of a hope that burned more slowly
than green hardwood in the fireplace.

Therefore, Harry, keep this spectrum,
this rainbowed pollen
in your pocket mirror,
when every lamp's been snuffed,
when hell is out dancing,
when a dark Lucifer lands
on a prow in the Thames, the Hudson, the Seine
and shakes his wings free of black pitch
and says: This is the hour.

There is no inheritance, no talisman
that resists the humid, hot summer wind
with the cobweb of memory.
(A story can only survive in ashes.
Tenacity is tantamount to destruction.)

Your sign was just.
One who has seen it cannot help but
find you. Everyone recognizes his own.

Your pride was not flight,
your humility by no means low,
the *black light* you lit somewhere far off
was not the rasp of a match.

LUCRETIUS

No one understands what sort of thing the soul is.
Is it already there in the fetus?
Or does the midwife fetch it
in the dew of the world?
Does it die instantly with us?
Or does it perish in the grave
and dissolve into the grass?
Or is there a region
where it has to go in the twilight,
or is it sent out again
as food and life for other livestock?

HIS PRAYERS

1

The slow cattle of my days
and all those years' resentment,
fretful romping in the neighbor's garden.

I dreamed I pulled off my eyelashes
and gave them to you, merciful one,
and you blew on them as on a dandelion,
oh, hold back your punishing hand!

In my subterranean shop of words
the iron squeezes, the plum tree bursts
and teeth release dry twigs.
Your consecrated bread will not heal me.

Nails, thorns, and the cloth of Veronica.
And how the entrails of the three murderers
on Golgotha shriveled up, even those of the third one!
Your will is done!

The veil of the temple comes unattached,
sinks over my gaze, my lips, my cross
through the intercession of all your mutilated children.

2

It is later than anyone can imagine.
What is there growing in our core?
What is gnawing at our spinal column?
We carry our skin.

      —Merciful One.

And we are not singed
while the darkness is already sinking
in the stairwell of thought
and night splits the bones of our fingers.

      —Look down in your mercy.

Warts of past misdeeds
are planted in the child
still dwelling inside its mother.
Quick. Push Father under the bed,
put on a crash helmet quick.

      —I submit
      to your pleasure.

3

The house rustles, a plank starts like a shot.
After which someone said my name,
close by, more clearly than my mother used to call it
in the evening street.

Clattering in leaves,
animals licking at water,
and my name, once again,
like a birch's bark bursting.

Listening to the muffled ticking
that quickens in my wrist
I wait for the order that will probably now
descend from a hellish flight of crows.

Demolish the house, stone by stone?
Staunch the fruit in her entrails?
What must I burn?
How to grease the prayer for good
that rattles in my bed?

4

The smooth sound of the angels
soothes the soldiers in the haze of the meadows
before they grope for their guns.
Ah, how sanctifying is Memlinc's piping,
the soldiers waltz.

>The day'll be dead
>as soldiers from lead
>as long as the sun can stand on its head.

>For us the cuckoo will call
>before Christ with stories that tall
>makes mincemeat of us all.

A soldier shrinks down into his collar.
—"They mustn't see my face,
them: them: the enemy!—I'm bleeding.

I'm so eager for the fray
I've bitten my cheek to pieces.
My bayonet is hotter than her thighs.

In the trenches crammed full of rags,
I know that soon only hair
and fingernails will be growing. But
that's all in the future. Before moss and thistles
run rampant in this tangible mist
I want to slit families' throats. So I can
smother the obscene noise of the litanies.
I do not want my eyes to blink
at God's wrath, nor at his love,
nor at his living life."

HIS NOTES FOR "GENESIS I.1"

It is not all that long ago,
The Jew pulled at the cart,
wrenched at the trees, hoisted and levered
and then staggered
  —and fell into the cart onto his father's corpse.

  (The cart in the garden in summer
  with rutabagas, dung, and hay
  is as innocent as your eyes.)

The dying Jew could not move the cart with the corpse,
the soldiers roared with laughter,
the enamel of their teeth did not burst.

In the sun, in a boulder, in the pupils of his beloved
man has discovered the circle
—he drew an axis and a circle around the animal in himself,
and to quiet the animal in himself,
—he built metal spokes and a cart big enough
for the bodies of his parents.

Do not talk about the natural hygiene of the universe
which justifies death.
The small death of love is not that of murder.

  (The cart is as guilty as your eyes.)

*

In the beginning was the word
and who has heard it?

A man stood still at the echo in his larynx
and gave voice to his fever

and sought in his audible speech
a construction for sword and scabbard.

Ever since, imagination goes on begging for murder.
The signal became definition.
The gristle listened,
the bronchiole spoke.

Mice were born out of an unwashed shirt.
Horsehairs soaked in water became worms.
Just as the sky is full of animals
the overflowing summer pressed
the word *heat* from our throat.

*

The language of fire?
Roasted vowels, singed sentences.
Boiling is a language. This morning in bed: the smell of coffee.

In the summer of 1944 the American Third Army destroyed
the cheese factories in Normandy—because of the smell—
the smell of corpses, the soldiers said.

In earlier times, Aristotle said, all meat was roasted.
It still is, wise man,
    you who said: "Socrates is pale"
    you who said: "Man begets mankind"
    you who already via concept,
               judgment,
               and reasoning,
    has found a solution
    for slaves and foundlings,

meat is still roasted
as in fairy tales: human flesh.

In the morning: the smell of coffee, the language of fire.
A burnt smell in the house, a complete lukewarmness.

THE MOTHER

I am not, I am only in your earth.
When you screamed and your skin quivered
My bones caught fire.

(My mother, caught in her skin,
Changes with the measure of the years.

Her eye is bright, escaped from the urge
Of the years through looking at me and
Calling me her happy son.

She was no stony bed, no animal fever,
Her joints were young cats,

But my skin remains unforgivable to her
And the crickets in my voice are motionless.

"You have outgrown me," she says dully
Washing my father's feet, and she is silent
Like a woman without a mouth.)

When you screamed my bones caught fire.
You put me down, I can't bear this picture again,
I was the invited but deadly guest.

And now, in my manhood I am strange to you.
You see me approach, you think: "He is
The summer, he makes my flesh and keeps
The dogs in me alive."

While you must die every day, apart
from me, I am not, I am not except in your earth.
In me your life dies in rotation, you do not
Return to me, from you I do not recover.

THE DEATH OF HIS ANCESTOR

Before his death he had already left us,
six months earlier, dull, broke, musty, broken,
although still whole he walked through our rooms.

"I have not had one moment of happiness,"
he said gasping audibly
for air in the kitchen air.

And then went blue. Like a plum.
He was fond of plums. All kinds,
preferably just ripe. Mother sat alone.

Not that he was dead then. No, he clung
to the chairs, seasick.
It was his heart that did not want to die,

the engine. The carcass, the chassis
were worn out but the engine was still good.
He stayed in bed and was sometimes dead.

The nuns hissed: "Yes, his time has come."
But a hiccup or two and he set off
again: only even bluer.

He was then taken to the room
that is reserved for dying—
where the soul escapes decay.

His head shrank visibly,
about the size of a woman's fist.
Eyes open. But can he still see?

It is nature. Had nothing more to eat
or drink. Though he still wanted to,
he chewed away. The nuns sang the Angelus.

When they wiped his lips with a
sponge, he bit on it and would not let go.
They pinched his nose and he let go.

No death rattle. The occasional hiccup.
Yes, his time has come. He was cold up to his knees
and his upper body was sweating. But the engine didn't stop.

They no longer washed him. Turning him over
would tip his heart over and cause it to stop.
Eau de cologne, not too strong, on his temples.

No loud talking. Nothing about debts. Nor
about a last signature. Go away, sir.
Son or no, go away. For he hears everything, everything.

His palate was black. His skin, don't speak of it.
With cotton wool the holes in his skin were rid
of the black that crept into the edges, so quickly.

Fist-sized craters in the jaws of his hole,
with black mould. Let out the clutch, a shock,
he raced the engine. Which stalled. Thank God.

And suddenly caved in.
The man-sized cavity within the truss
was filled up with cardboard and cotton wool.

Straightened out, otherwise he'll stay bent
and his bones will have to be broken.
He must be laid out fine. Everyone will be seeing him.

No more washing now either. Any contact
disperses the flesh, light as pollen in spring.
In the holes: the bonemeal of his fishbones.

Then came the troublesome distress for Sir Wild Boar,
Inundated with family council and solicitor.
And the time of the hearse and the funeral.

I was the nail in his coffin, he often said.
Now just a fingernail, as a parting gesture
scratching against the walnut of his head.

Lord, take your son into your arms.
The women went on the left (all loved ones)
The men on the right (all sons).

Time of the earth which now ferments in him.
Time of the seasons. A pint of beer, quick.
Many ancestors—and all disinherited.

ELEPHANT

I came upon that elephant
soaked to the skin by the rain. "Hello, beast."—"Hello, sir."

We became good friends, as one does.
I get along with long-nosed animals and those with trunks.
He found me, I believe, somewhat fearful.
I, on the other hand, was charmed by his sweet nature.
And also by his majesty,
for isn't the elephant the emblem of the world,
four pillars propping up a globe of anthracite?

Often, when the moon was full, as sometimes happens,
he would waft coolness at me
a young birch in his trunk,
as if I were the King of Palms.

And then one day (why? I'd done nothing wrong!)
I caught him giving me a look.
An ice-cold look, a plaice's look,
no pity there of any guise
in those round tinny eyes.

Then I put on my wishing cloak
I donned my wig of cunt-hair
and topped it with my dreaming cap
with circles, stars, and stripes,
and then I recited my formula of murder
from the Catalogue of Changeable Signs.
The elephant was an instant corpse.
Without a sigh he fell on his rump,
and rumbled, crumbled, tumbled into ash,
and the ash in the grass shot upward
in a different form, that of an oleander.
Which I cut off at the roots.

Which now stands beautiful beside me on my terrace
glinting and stinking. But there is
something that I miss, I don't know what it is,
but I do not want to look for it again.

DANTE AND I

I

On Thursday the 14th of September, Dante's birthday,
I was strolling in my garden, the dusk was mild
and I was thinking of Dante.
That's how I am, I'm always thinking of Dante.
There's something of the man in me, I think. I'm as moderate as
he is.

II

Then winged mastiffs landed in a whoosh of sulphur
and feathers and barking right at my feet.
Dammit, right out of a fragment of a Canto,
this mess flopped down on my lawn
and scrabbled around and squealed in a hateful tangle,
nothing less than a nightmare,
the feathers flew over to the neighbors
among all their miniature windmills and garden gnomes.
Then, suddenly, they were gone. Like a vision from Dante.

III

Now, that really wasn't called for.
Really, such a frenzy,
that splatter of claws and wings, the screeching
and the stench that clung to my clothes for weeks after,
I'm a civilized man, I didn't ask for that.

Above all, and this is the point, my cellphone
got caught in the fray, was how to put it? mutilated
and crushed and then devoured.

I had built it myself, à la Calder, simply,
out of aluminum, in primary colors,
a triangle, a circle, and a square, nothing more,
and yet it happened also to be everything,
I had called it my "Universe,"
for the triangle represents the body, right?
physically, orally, and mentally,
the square: water and air and fire and earth,
and the circle, simply, you know,
ultimate reality.
The three elements cut out of aluminum, strung together with
        wire,
I had painted pink, a touch of salmon,
a hint of corset rose.

IV

As I said to the police officers: "These lawless
beasts have utterly
ruined and devoured a piece of work
in which I have in-vest-ed years of handiwork
as well as the expression of my soul and my ethics.
And who, gentlemen, can ever make amends for this?"

"Sir," a policeman said, "the infinite
contains in itself many formless elements."

They took down my complaint. Complaint
against an unknown quantity
with an infinite digestion.

I hate my offspring and my wife.
Dante alone consoles my life.

THEATER

How busily and yet unbodily
they strut with the air of the stage
in their beards! How they try out
what on the spot they imitate
a life that prattles out of their costumes,
that rustles along the patient boards!

In a plot full of hooks and eyes
on the existence or nonexistence of God
they blare notes of compassion and scorn and
what we hear is seven tame rabbits in a hutch.

One steps forward and says:
"I am Laertes, robbed of my sister,"
and thinks "I am John so-and-so
and my brain is a blister."

Ophelia sobs sullenly,
a chicken still squawking
and then drowning in evil.

Horatio bungles his cue bewitched
by elocution lessons.
Oppressed by a death applauded by few
he bungles his lines
and heavily slaps grease-painted flanks.

In the dressing room Claudius gives a pin-up a kiss.
In the wings Polonius reads *The People's Paper*.
Fortinbras is standing having a piss
against the Belfort tower—he only comes on later.

The rigid cadences, the curt calls,
Silenced each day for the time being!
The First Player never flaps at all,
he comes forward and thinks: "Thank God
I am not who I am. Give me a part,
a name, so to myself I may remain unknown."

Listen to the wind in cardboard sails.
Observe the blooms of the polyester grass
and how the queen lies burning with desire
on her incestuous mattress.

Fortunately all this lightweight liberal
mumbling will every hour be shattered and
pulverized by the clanging of the
bells from Saint Bavo's cathedral.

And who comes forward then and says:
"At last the day has dawned,"
and says to his mother in the front row:
"At last, mummy, the day is done"?

He, Prince Hamlet, stuttering commuter,
limping wish dream, a despised and
well-loved, lousy, gadabout orphan who,
though clouds of sleep are seeping from the ridge,
reeks for many a long night,
until the final curtain and the final bow.

A STRANGE DAY

Sometimes quickly forgotten, preferably never thought
about, the bodies hit by napalm.
Or even worse, believing
that it is always the same, something
like a law—like the Wars of the Roses.

And to read instead on the john
about the *lineaments of desire*
in this unworldly day.
This submersion is called suppression.

Ah, the Tivoli gardens
    (Tibur, Tubure, Tibori, Tivori, Tivoli)
and eating beans, Pythagoras' favorite food.
Armored cars flatten the graves in the grass.

Your left breast: sweet, your right: salt.
In the palm of your left hand: love
and in your right palm the same.

Do acolytes sometimes spit in the blood of God?
Rams sniff each other, draw back,
run at each other, batter their skulls,
a shot, a woman sinks into the rice paddy.

Seeing and hearing, it is an illness.
Speaking and saying are two, the speaker says.
That song again. I have never loved you.
I will always love you.

THE STRESS-WORD: HOUSE

Loneliness is a dwelling.
(A dwelling encloses—warm

Houses a season in rooms and
Becomes a face—soft

Is loneliness and ripens in-
Tently from child to man and corpse.)

Do not be like a dwelling.
Love is a cramp, and

(A murder) lunges for an
Instant: a tyrant that dies, a splitting conch.

Mirrors ripen. Do not be like a mirror.

*

A little earth
And the border of the chalky sea
Over which a starving bird hovers
Are what the man walks on.

The sand moves,
The branches of the wood: gone
Into the branches of the sky.
What estate does the man attain?

He sings where
She swells—her helmet and her fur
Are hard—only the field along
Her heart gives way.

THE WEATHER

What was the weather like in the country without you?
First fog descended
over the concrete mountains.

Then the sun hung like mist
over the mother-of-pearl sand.

Then the air moved
and became as clammy as your armpits.

Sheet lightning made my teeth clench.

And everywhere the smell rose
of huge animals that do not exist

except in the rushing of your ears,
in the rustling of your hair.

That was the weather there without you.
You were the air pressure and the dew
and the snow in my skull.

I WRITE YOU DOWN

My wife, my heathen altar,
That I play and caress with fingers of light,
My young wood that I overwinter,
My neurotic, unchaste, and tender emblem,
I write your breath and your body down
On lined music paper.

And against your ear I promise brand-new horoscopes
And prepare you once more for world travels
And for a sojourn in some Austria or other.

But by gods and constellations
Eternal happiness also grows mortally weary,
And I have no house, I have no bed,
I do not even have any birthday flowers for you.

I write you down on paper
While you swell and blossom like a July orchard.

SIMPLE

That you should be what's evil
and I, don't make me laugh, what's good,
or vice versa,
don't make me laugh,
the two of us dance on just one leg.
When I kneel at your knees
and when I bring you to your knees
we are fragments full of pity and danger
for each other.
With chains around their necks
the dogs of love come.

LOVE ME OR LEAVE ME

With a motto: "love me or leave me,"
with a vulva full of semolina, milk teeth, fruit,
with one shaky leg on the earth,
with glassy, hazy, crazy longings,
with virtues out of the garbage can of the West,
with the one shaky, oy, oy, that puss of a foot
that strokes my temple and gropes for the earth,
botched together with flaps and laps,
with that lover of hers who no longer phones her
(which explains her vegetable, vindictive conk
after bonking) (on that speckled graceful Egyptian body)
with hunks and worms of quicklime wishes
with the sadness of the small independent one,

is it not beastly
that of all those I have desired
she remains most dear to me,
she who deserted?

A WOMAN

With twittering hair,
With gull's eyes, with a pouch on her belly,
A mother or a good betrayer,
Who knows this blazing woman?

Her nails approach my wood,
Her claw-pain wakes my skin,
Like a hunting horn she hangs tingling in my hair.

She approaches in folds and in lightning flash,
In heat, in resin, in rattling,
While in a state of desire,
Stretched like a gun and
In a state of attack and of murder I
Envelop, plow, and cut down,
Bending, kneeling, the odorous animal
Between the leather-soft knees.

She splits my cone
In the familiar heat.

*

I would like to sing you a song in this landscape of rage,
Livia, one that would penetrate you, reach you in your nine
    openings,
Blond and elastic and hard.

It would be an orchard song and a song of the plain,
A one-man chorus of shame,
As if my vocal chords disbanded arose from me and called
    you,
As if
In this landscape that humiliates me, in this dwelling that
    damages me
(In which I wander on all fours) we no longer appeared
    unequal
And closed our voices.
Arise in offshoots,
Draw near to me who am not to be approached,
Do not be strange to me as the earth is,

Do not flee from me (the cripples)
Meet me, feel me,
Bend, break, break,

We are the crosswind, the rain of days,
Tell me clouds,
Flow open wordless, become water.

(Ah, this light is cold and presses its callused hands
Into our face that falters and folds up)

I would like to sing you an orchard song, Livia
But the night becomes complete and fills

My plain ever more tightly tight—I cannot reach you
Except unfulfilled
For the stag's throat clogs as dawn comes.

STILL

It was another time,
I want to forget it.
In other alleyways.
We wanted to and could. But didn't dare.
It was for life. We were afraid.

We became a chronic illness
for each other.
And then we slowly froze
fox-trotting among the dead.

Until the day I kissed her carotid
and, over her left shoulder
in the trees saw Orion,
the blind hunter who grinned
and then pointed at us and called his dogs.

And our soul of love
with its misery and moaning
fell to pieces,
spread out over our days past.
It was another time.
Dull rain in other alleyways.

OF THE GROUND

Of the cold ground
of the May in me
of her (as a blueprint) on my cataract
of sunburn in the no-man's-land of the bed
I peel

Of the clover between the corpse's ribs
I tell
and of the damned dull days
when I could please her
with a refrain on her lukewarm hair

of how I came from the ground
to her mouth

SONNETS

I

That for a single moment most things are designed
to gain perfection only to die out,
reflects the will of both the world and Einstein.
And that people are like leaves that sprout

under pollution filling every sky
and within memory that they fade alike
is guaranteed by time, which I detect
clutching me by the scruff of the neck.

Therefore, at my wits' end, I'm called
upon at one moment to laud
the fact that I see you on display,

your young magic as not seen before,
a naked monument that unpunished falls
forward, toppling before my gaze.

II

If in the occident there's nothing new
just what's been there from the word go,
what then can I invent that, wrongly too,
some infant did not think long ago?

Etruscan, Aztec, and Hellenic—as such
you're pinned as postcards on the wall and hung—
ogled, for sale and worshipped far too much,
my centuries-old shrew forever young.

How would the ancient world react
to your body's present miracle?
Go on believing that no instant will

ever return unless the memory's intact?
The old rogues simply were unable
to handle your self-containment—nor can I still.

III

I thought (a dog's my frequent guise):
"I'll wait until the wintertime is here,
that can etch lines around her mouth in a trice,
or until cunning spring that envies her

and plows deep furrows in her skin's fine field,
and then she'll be as I am, marred at best.
Suddenly though this autumn was here, its yield
bewildering and blessed

like my late love and you remain unscathed,
my love. I dare to state my creed
that my coldness will never be your death,

that you will never leave me, dazed
by my deep-freeze breath.
I believe so. As do corpses that still bleed.

IV

What you desire, what you refuse, what you may be,
assumes the many shadowy strange curves
of a stranger in my tent and she
has a horrible effect on my nerves,

the unshakable merry widow, she looks
like all her shadows shown on spec.
Do you give me too the selfsame looks?
Aggrieved, I learn I look just like your ex.

My metaphors are where I then take flight.
Shadows that rhyme, for me that's easy.
Rhetorically, for example: that you taste of spring grass,

or illogically: that you bend like wheat,
or typically: that of late your upper lip was
as lewd as the down of your pussy.

V

Saw a steaming gray that stood there damp
when the sky sucked water from its mane.
Saw a black cloud lick a rainbow clean.
Saw flamingos, flying dogs, starvation camps.

Saw only yesterday how undefiled
though spattered by sunlight the wet lawn gleamed,
it was as if, it could just be, it seemed
to be the iris of your eyes, now multiplied,

and I forgot all space, all speech, all text,
And at a phantom insect I lashed out
as at your image.

Since you my gaze is all bewitched,
Even more shattering have I brought about
and mended not one fragment of the damage.

VI

Singing in the shower just over you.
My common sense for once not acting daft.
Suddenly, in mid-handstand, I just knew
that you're my identical better half

and that we therefore, quite serene,
would do much better living far apart.
It sounds quite common, possibly obscene,
but only then can I give you your part.

Absence would only start to gnaw me through
if I were not to think of you as one
that brings together all my abaci.

Therefore I honor distance and the night alone,
the only way to make your one a two,
the two desires alive, unsatisfied.

VII

That I love my own ego far too much, well sure, all right,
and that it is a sin to taint your soul this way
and that it is an illness which, day and night,
lays waste the ego till it wants to die?

Okay, so what? A mirror as my measure
may I then dance till all my notes are known?
I've realized too late and with no pleasure
that I'm farsighted, and I own

that's why I've never managed properly
to master my defeat at every turn.
Besides, that's what I decide for you,

especially when blindly riding you.
Only what you would seek to read in me
will I still learn.

VIII

Just now my stomach clenched with spite
and I don't know, by God, why I feel so.
Don't lie, friend. It was only something trite
and it's envy that controls your glands too.

Why, for example, is William rich and why
does Francis have those sea-green eyes of his
and why is John Disaster always right
and why must I put up with all of this?

Love, tell me that I need not get fret up
and make of misery such heavy weather,
that I must sing freely like a lark,

each morning of our blazing time together
when, between the sheets, we're both set up
after the cries, yawns, sobbings in the dark.

IX

Once more alone in my nest, badly worn,
She lies reviving with that other man, it seems.
I travel in my head, in all the corn
and chaff of my dreams.

My dreams drag themselves forward on their knees.
They mill-sail toward her
like hordes of sightless men on skis,
they make so many blunders, such disorder

that there her shadow starts to gleam.
Like amber. Like the gray dawn
she makes the black unblack

and I cannot calm down, I claw
toward the bright spot of her heart, back
toward that light that simply will not dim.

X

You want freedom? Forget it, lady,
you've got no talent for it, no antenna,
you have no taste for freedom's Gehenna,
nor for its pain, nor for the remedy.

Don't lose yourself in the monotone
of sleep indifferent to sleeping,
in fiddling at that erogenous zone
all with its flowing and its gaping.

Pretend instead in fetters you're restrained
and after screwing whisper about being free,
blame me as the one who is enslaving

and let me be deluded, let me be,
tumbling in your moonstruck raving
in one contentment tightly chained.

XIV

And when the little copper kettle full
of the ashes I once was is emptied out
over the patient grass, my beautiful,
don't stand around and fool about

wiping the mascara from your cheeks.
Think of the fingers which once wrote these lines
when our longing was at its peak
and which stroked you when they were still alive.

And laugh at what I was—recalling then
the cinema and that snoring spate,
the parts that always used to tug

the feeble joke and lumbering gait
toward you time and time again
when I had your now warm lushness, in the bag.

XV

Years ago I was able to dream
(oh infantile, prophetic soul)
of things as yet unseen,
fatal as the invention of the wheel.

Now the world is mortal just like me,
and that's the end of it.
My only kick is from uncertainty,
I don't believe in shit.

Dreams I chase up to the attic
where the stupid children live.
I'm lying. There is still one lunatic

idea for which in this pious sonnet
I provide a narrative—
one last demon with my name on it.

TOUSSAINT LOUVERTURE

Behind my back the whites lay in the coach's velvet
and I drove the grays and learned
numbers, thoughts, and how black I was.
Then I fled into the familiar forest
and formed regiments there and murdered and vanquished.
Later, leader and emperor,
I suffered from an "excess of moderation."
(Balance, composure, the roster of the whites.)
That was the fall, my fall.

Now, molded in matchless gold,
proof against acids and alkalis,
in the rind of my regalia,
with cilia of brilliant lead, joints of copper pyrites,
with too many toes and a harelip,
with bendable, crushable cartilage,
with minerals as glands,
I am a disturbance in history,
a defenseless Gloria.

The woolly-haired monkey resists now
in a niche of pity.

TANCREDO INFRASONIC

Enough I say to the house
Which stands between night and morning

Enough to the alphabet of licorice
To the tame and colorful animal of sounds

I have thought enough about words
And this poem is no poem

No secret cellar no barred face
This is a letter to my brother this is driftwood
A Message to the population a friendly
Saying addressed to a soldier

    "In the absence of a guitar
    of a lute and of emotion
    of money and of happiness
    in the absence of hate of wound fever and of spleen
    in the absence of love and of happiness (second time)
    but with a raging song in a body not to mention
    in holy misery

let us look at the tree as it unfolds
the woman who becomes pregnant
the dream that blue as highland
splits like a tree
the rain that writes ETCETERA on our face
that is neither dead nor alive but answers
like an automaton that breathes:

in the absence of *et a capo*"

*

The doors of time no longer shut
And father and mother have deceived

We learn 1 and 1 and a and b aybee
How one should burn down houses of shame
How one hits friends and enlightens women
How without sins without virtues
Without ice and without fire
One remains white and untouched
Like a round cobblestone by the sea
We learn (but we hope forlornly)
We learn (but we think bookishly)

We learn: Morning is a chicken that sits on Easter Island eggs
The world is open to children
Evening is a cock on account of thrice Peter

But learn afterward: Morning is always an evening
On account of the hundred times three times everyday
        betrayal
For not a single Last Supper
For not a single piece of silver

And learn: Love does not conquer
Love does not conquer any more
And wake our house any more
Our house any more
Like the cock earlier in the farmhouse room

ULYSSES

I have seen too much fighting,
heard too much whining of suitors,
I have always journeyed too far.

A peep-show has replaced my eye
a spinning-top my ear.

Too much mire,
too many carrion in it.
Too much joy.

I now conceal myself among the lovers,
those beggars.

BITTER TASTES

Bitter tastes the herb of memory.

Cannons, phosphorus rocks,
Chalk stubble-rapes surround my dwelling and who
Does not stand guard there, unchaste sentries for the sign
Of the blackberry brake, of the horn,
Of the helmeted weathercock of hate?

One step and spider monkeys glide
Slide in on fingers
And make a path in the pause of my blood. And live there
fast
And live there slow. Until it burns in the hay of all words,
Until it burns in the past field, the drunken days and
Their fermenting grain.

BEFORE THE GATE

That routine should be peaceful
I have long believed, a peace of branches and
snails. Just as senseless sculptured sentences
should calm disorder. But I am the rhythm,
dented, sealed, held together
by wires that cannot be knotted
in that ever dingier light
of forms
as assumptions.

The forms are slight as fragments,
but despite this link the things.
The things faint
when someone recognizes them, giving rise
to memories, the color, the cloud, the street,
the man who wobbles on his bike into nothingness.
Nothingness? Worms
on your blanket.

Skimming through the air, the falling flames
which through a light-fall change into yellow rain
or, if you wish it, golden tongues,
shreds of great absences, of prayers
that should plug every hole. For what reasons?
For what we did together?
Stretch out your hand.
For all that.

For, dismal as it may be, the latch opens dream's door
into the black forest of assumptions.
Spectral streaks of blood flow
and yet no coat, no grass is spattered.
The world will grow pale whether there was unity
or balance or not,
without a signal,
from within.

Do you recognize your fellow-man, the fellow coughing
with his back to you, away from your bestialities?
He is looking elsewhere, for presences
outside your moment, that dependent, temporal
monument, for reasons you could hear
if you only listened.
But you continue to rot in discord
in your coat of gold-leaf lies.
Discord before a gate
is what your ear hears.

Perhaps she is the only one there, the faithful one.
Not grieving for things, she imagines
and she is the earth. From behind her window she looks
for the struck back, the grim shoulders,
the pillory of the man. The time of the man,
wine and vinegar, is not her time. That looking of hers
is the time of the earth. She, the faithful one, waits
and laughs at the shadows that stand up
against the rims of the world. She says:
"To be present, that is enough."

STELE

I

Although dispersed and finally destroyed by reason
they yet remain alive, those moments that you order
into something like an existence.
However much you want to forget and lose, it is too much
    to ask,
a non-existence, odd traces are left over.
What we learn when seeking for a being between soul
and skin is the law: clear off!
If we had been able to choose between man or stone,
    oh then,

                                oh then ...
But the wretch chose to be a man, that will teach him.

Hence the dragon temples, the temple of concord and
that of music. Man, what have we not built
and piled up: stones for all the others!
Hence the buildings always embellished for their own good
    with
their caryatids, busts, palms, pilasters, for the soul, for

                                the form,
for the others. Crazy about the droll dictate: the relationship
is more than the ornament.

Meanwhile, pondering practically how to split oak
(look at shipbuilding) along the pith-rays
of the outline, inward, toward the center.
Meanwhile, the general chiselling in marble and chests of
    drawers, in the
late-romanesque ashtray, in the Louis Quinze bedstead.

From the corner where the child with ass's ears stands
the past weaves its web and darkens the day.
How long can we not scheme above the earth of our
dreams?
Is that a bird or a turd in the form of a bird?
Sit down, man, and stretch your neck for the bullet.

II

Far away, in trailers, in containers
people lie cradled against each other
like teaspoons.

You think that you alone are rotting
deep in your ornamented grottoes
with your face of an uninvited guest
among the ghastly alabaster and the common
roses (your translation of snow and fire),
you, translator, foolish son of man
who like the light that conjures colors
stays colorless itself.

Should, must nature, knowledge, identity
form an ever newer world?
Are we extensions of each other?
Do you yourself believe it?
Nail your door shut without delay.

III

A piece of furniture supports (its animal form).
Or stows away (its architecture).
The chair is a horse's back,
the cupboard's a coffin.

The chair, lonely as man,
sculpture of firewood,
obscure extension of the wall,
a play on itself,
gradually decays like you
into regulated slothfulness.
Its seat: a memory of a horse's big bones,
its back an imitation of my own. The chair must stand
and you must move
for rest and fever lead equally
to transition, to destruction.
Now you must move,
before you gradually become the last one
and are placed against the wall,
a *ployant*, a *tabouret de grâce*
waiting there until it is loved,
that is, until someone sits on it.

IV

Whether in that godforsaken given time on earth nothing
sticks? Whether we see things or only have the
sensation of seeing? Shut down like televisionary Beirut?
Sew your eyelids tight or not, the soul goes bankrupt.
I hear you say: "I refuse to recognize anything except on the
evidence of my eyes."
But eyes fail,
each day clouds the avid lens that remains fixed
on the battlefield, on so much violence.

Leibniz says that the simple things have no windows
looking at each other, but only exist for each other
for there is unity somewhere
if only in the eye of God. That's nothing to me.
Give me Vico, who says that by means of a colossal
ignorance, *in una corpolentissima fantasia*
we pretend. And thus act and create.

Something like a human must have existed once,
for he disappears before our very eyes, shriveled,
immersed and still inclined to supervise
his body, surprised by stories of creation,
scourged by the neurons that course through brain pan
and that translate handy hints for his internal television.

And the nature which we rule over becomes vocabulary and
composition, homesickness for something known by no one.
Every house a grave, sure, but, darling,
furnished even so with fragments of a rainbow.
Our house: a railroad car on frozen tracks.
We will survive. Our house is built on a rock.
The windows are of rock.

DESCRIPTION

Into a world of clouds
He stepped with his case full of waves,
His mouth full of her hair,
An unangular man who listened
To the noises of people from the middle class
And then his teeth chattered, he almost sniveled,
Though mostly his tears froze.
(The heart of a woman and a glowworm
burn wordlessly.)
Don't look at me—that gives me hives.
Sporadically consistent,
A restless protoplasm
That limply laughed about the woman who danced on one leg.
Suspicious of every true-to-life
Choreography—that bobbing, badgering, prancing, squeaking
Seems too much to him, so he snickered
At what swells, festers, flows, splutters, gurgles,
Man without clothes
In the time that glides earthward.
All too carelessly wobbling through the hourglass,
Much too mocking since sometimes copying the courtiers
      around him
Who glisten from the oil of sardines and kings,
All too greedy imagining himself as a mammal,
Powerful and fragile like a Boeing.
His dead mother sniffed at him
As if at a freshly starched shirt.
His now-passed past? With creaking spokes,

Busted butt, on the trampoline, on the beach,
In the niche of the cathedral
He got off the ground,
Never idyllically horizontal.
Often setting off for distant blue mountains
But inside a picture postcard.
Peacock-like? That, too. Because he knew he'd been created
For the void, his feathers claimed his attention,
Feathers that burn with his adolescent secrets.
Now really, young man, really.
His dead mother said: "Paper is patient."
Yet he wrote in the age of a line and a fart
Imitating a decorative death
The inventory of his feigned history.
He was often moved around, in each house
He cast a white shadow. Mostly smaller.
Like all wise men he died from anger.
Probably his teeth chattered, listening
To a choir in the spring foolish as love.
"Nymphs and Shepherds, dance no more."

ETUDE

There is, there is so much, for example, the unhappy man
who stands describing in the summerhouse.
He describes values, complementary colors
the disturbance in the spheres
the glaze of the pluperfect tense.

There is the teacher and his total history
there is the Jesuit of the straight line
the poulterer of the transient
the man who breakfasts with a concept
the man who swallows aleatorically
the man who sobs in cold-storage cellars about
the ever more fugitive paradox of space
the man who lives by the obscene laws of art

while *ex nihilo*

There is that which emerges out of thirst
there is that which is undone by that emergence
there is nature with her edges and loose ends
there is pigment and the trace of a hoof
there is something silent like a steaming hill
something wild like the dirt of distress
there is a ladder beneath the branches
there is the madness of the leaves
the calm of the flames
there is Eris who roams
in search of the lamentations of man
there are the corpses of friends

there is *ex nihilo*
anyway the heavy weather
and the nearby tumult of the distant sea.

HUNT FOR MERCY

I want to stay in love
until the beginning of September.
After that I will keep you
(as Idi Amin did the twelve heads of
his enemies) in the fridge.
All flesh is grass but already
the fear that was me evaporates
in the face of "the sea with tresses"
(said Archilochus who was in a position to know).
And the angels that were to descend in hordes
to celebrate (Club Bruges, a birth
an operation) and then to flee back
in the dark?
I did not see them. Blind for you.
Somewhere you are laughing away,
somewhere beneath the unseen stars,
in this wry poem.

BROTHER

"It's hard," he said, "bloody hard.
And unfair, for the first time I'm getting thin."

Still autumn outside, a field of maize to the skyline,
the word falls, skyline, finite.
Then no other word from him.

In his gullet the plastic tube.
He hiccups for hours on end. Cannot swallow.

Still, movement in the right hand,
which holds the left one like a greasy lily.
The hand stretches its thumb upward.
He keeps on signaling into his final decline.

He has white child-skin.
He squeezes my fearful hand.

I'm still looking for a resemblance, ours,
her restlessness,
his impatience (no time for time).
the distrust and credulity of both of them
and I land in our earliest past,
the world as a meadow with frogs,
as a ditch with eels
and later bets, Ping-Pong,
household rules, the fifty-two cards,
the three dice

and all the time that unbridled hunger.
(I grow old instead of you.
I eat pheasant and smell the woods.)

His dwelling is now measured.
The machine breathes for him.

Slime is siphoned off.
A rattle from his diaphragm,
and then his last movement, a slow wink.

Transmigration of souls. An arrangement. A portion cut off.
The body still diminishing
and then suddenly in his face that was dead
a frown and a spasm
and then a wide-open, wild look,
unbearably clear, the anger and terror
of a tyrant. What does he see? Me, a man
who turns away, a coward surprised at his tears?
Then it is morning and the straps are loosened.
And he then for good.

ROBERT DESMET

He has seen the distant mountains
and the village close by.
The music forest misses its faun,
its alchemist.

He believed in gods
and in their secrets
just as he believed
in human dreams.

Gods, embrace your child,
for we did so too little.
Embrace this courtly youth.

OSTEND

There, my life started to decay.
I was nineteen, I slept
In the Hôtel de Londres on the top floor.
The mail boat passed beneath my window.
Each night the town consigned itself
To the waves.

I was nineteen, I played cards
With fishermen on the Iceland run.
They came from the Great Cold
Their eyes and lashes caked with salt, and
Bit into chunks of
Raw pork.
Ah, the click of dice. In those days
Of darts and diceboards I always won.

Then at dawn past the cathedral,
The stone cocoon of fear,
Along the deserted dike, the Kursaal.
The all-night bars
With the hollow-eyed croupiers,
The bankrupt bankers,
English girls with TB.
And from the turquoise sea
The cruel screech of gulls.
"Come in, Mister Wind,"
Yells an excited child
And over Ostend swirls a cloud of sand

From the invisible other shore
Hazy England
And the Sahara.

Past the shop windows of pharmacists who back then
Sold condoms under the counter
Past the pier and the breakwaters,
The fish market with its sea monsters,
The race course where one Sunday
I stopped winning.

Sundays that came and went.
Nights in the Hotel of the Spas
Where I started at her moaning,
Sighing, singing.
Her sound still scourges
My memories.
I have known other islands,
Seas, deserts—Istanbul, that castle in the air,
Chiang-Mai with its land mines,
Zanzibar in the heat of cinnamon,
The slow, sluggish Tagus. They
Steadily disappear.

Sharper in the light of the north
I see the childlike face
Of the Master of Ostend ensconced in his beard.
He was made of gristle,
Then of wax,
Now of bronze.
The bronze in which he
Smiles at his stone-dead youth.

WHAT TO SPEAK ABOUT

What to speak about tonight? And what to preach
in a land we recognize, tolerate,
seldom forget.
That country with its droll beginnings,
its clammy climate, its sapless stories
about the old days,
its inhabitants, greedy till their final fall
among the cauliflowers.
They keep on multiplying
in a paradise of their own imagining,
hankering for happiness, shivering, mouths full of porridge.
Just as in nature—
while depilating our puny hills,
scorching our pastures, poisoning our air,
the guileless cows graze on.

Speak about the writings of this land,
printed matter full of question marks
on the patient paper
which time and again is shocked by its history
and so resorts to concealing shorthand.
Speak about the curtains
that people draw around themselves.
But still we hear them, the stinking
primates that stalk each other in rooms.
Just as in nature—
the hibiscus gives off no scent,
while the innocent cows do, bogging down
in the piss-logged earth.

Speak in that land of glittering grass
in which man,
intemperate worm, dreaming carcass,
dwells among the corpses which dead as they are
remain obedient to our memory.
Just as our nature expects a single,
simple miracle that one day will finally
explain what we were,
not just this remote spectacle
time has thrown together.

Speak about that time which, they said,
would mark us like a brand and palimpsest?
We lived in an age of using
and being usable.
What defense against that?
What festive feathers in the ass?
What cellar song? Perhaps.
Say it. Perhaps.
A few swift scratches in slate
and there's the outline of your love.
Fingerprints in the clay are her hips.
Syllables of joy sometimes sounded
if she, when she, called you like a cat.

Speaking about her presence
wakens the blue hour of twilight.
Just as in nature,
the merciless, glassy, blue azure
of our planet seen from Apollo.

And though from simply speaking
your headdress begins to feel heavy
and the lifeline in your palm
begins to throb
still, nevertheless,
honor the flowering
of the shadows that inhabit us,
the shadows begging for consolation.
And still stroke her shoulder blade.
Like the back of a hunchback
hankering for a ferocious happiness.

SUMMER

Suddenly those three months
with nothing but drought.

The cypresses with their reddish brushes,
The white venomless scorpion.

A summer of burnt paper.
Nature keeps on gabbling
while I rot.

Then you came
and since then I am
short of hands and eyes
and tongue-tied.